NOTES FROM
THE SONG OF LIFE

NOTES FROM THE SONG OF LIFE

Spiritual Reflections by Tolbert McCarroll

Celestial Arts
Millbrae, California

DEDICATED
TO
TAMAR and DUNCAN

and all the other
children who will
be a part of
the Story

First printing: May, 1977
Manufactured in the United States of America

Library of Congress Cataloging in Publication Data

McCarroll, Tolbert.
  Notes from the song of life.

  1. Meditations. I. Title
BV4832.2M16   242'.4   77-7135
ISBN 0-89087-200-7

1 2 3 4 5 6 7 — 83 82 81 80 79 78 77

Contents

Wherever the path leads
I will follow.
Wherever the road goes
I will walk.

To the Reader . . .

This is a book of inner dialogues which I want to share with others who are as spiritually stubborn as I am. These pieces were written down over a seventeen-month period. They came as interior urgings, usually early in the morning following a day during which I had engaged in intensive spiritual direction with a group or individual. At first I was reluctant to share these writings because of the stern tone in some of them. Then I realized that I was the one who was being guided and corrected by these words. Gradually I began to read some of these pieces aloud in my own Community and in sessions on spiritual growth at various centers in Canada and the United States. Other people seemed to find these words relevant and helpful. After reflection I decided to publish them.

Somehow when I began the book I knew there would be thirty chapters. When the thirtieth one was written I experienced an immediate detachment from the work. All that was coming had been launched.

THE USE OF THIS BOOK

The author of the 14th Century mystical text on spiritual formation, THE CLOUD OF UNKNOWING, charged the reader not to allow the work to fall into the hands of any except those who were seriously committed to a spiritual path. He or she went on to say:

> I charge you and I beseech you by the authority of love, that if any shall read, write or speak of this book, that you charge them as I do you, for to take time to read it, speak it, write it, or hear it all over. For it may be there is some matter in the beginning, or in the middle, the which is hanging, and not fully explained where it stands. If it be not dealt with there, it is soon after, or else at the end. Wherefore, if a person saw one matter and not another, it may lead lightly to error. Therefore, in eschewing this error, both in yourself and in all other, I pray you for love to do as I say you.
>
> As for fleshly janglers, open praisers and blamers of themselves or others, tellers of trifles, grumblers, tattlers of tales and all manner of pinchers—cared I never that they saw this book. For mine intent was never to write such thing unto them, and therefore I would that they meddle not therewith; and let it be the same for all those who are merely curious, be they learned or unlearned.

This present work is also presented only to those who are earnestly attempting to live spiritual lives and it will have little relevance to anyone else.

I strongly urge you not to read more than one chapter a day. This book provides the framework for a month of reflections.

Precede and follow the reading with silence. This should be done even though a particular chapter may be read and reread several times during the day. Thus your experience will be like a sandwich, and the little bits that are presented in this book are put between two thick slices of your own nutritious quiet.

All writers and readers of inner dialogue should be warned by the wise and sobering words of St. John of the Cross:

> And I am appalled at what happens in these days— namely, when some soul with a penny's worth of medi- tation experience, if it be conscious of certain locutions of this kind in some states of recollection, at once chris- tens them all as coming from God. . . . This happens very commonly, and many persons are greatly deceived by it, thinking that they have attained to a high degree of prayer and are receiving communications from God. Wherefore, they either write this down or cause it to be written, and it turns out to be nothing, and to have the substance of no virtue, and it serves only to encourage them in vanity.

There is nothing original in this work. More than once I have discovered in an ancient text an almost identical statement to one that I had written here. Furthermore, I know that my reading in spiritual literature often resulted in concepts being uncon- sciously stored away for this later use.

However, I do not believe that the thoughts pre- sented here originated with any other writers. Any wisdom in these words has been and will always be available to all people at all times in our Story. From time to time there are instruments for bringing some of these concepts to life in a new age or to a new audience or even to one person who has not pre- viously heard them. Some of the instruments are self-free and pure. Others are awkward.

I recognize the influence of a number of teachers from my readings and reflections. At the head of the list are the ancient Taoist masters, and particularly the authors of the TAO TE CHING and the CHUANG TZU. Next come the 14th Century Western mystics sometimes called the "Friends of God." From that sparkling company two stand out as having a particular influence on this present work, Dame Julian of Norwich and Meister Eckhart. There are a number of places in these words where I can see the hands of the Egyptian desert monks of the early Christian church, especially St. Anthony and St. Evagrius. Finally, there is the tradition of the Chinese Zen masters, particularly as their spiritual lineage was transmitted to Japan by Dogen and then to the Western world in the life and the words of the late Shunryu Suzuki-Roshi. Now these are all good teachers, but they must not be blamed for the shortcomings of a lazy and inattentive student turned author.

PICTURES

The photographs were taken by Sister Mary Martha and myself. We are both members of the Community of the Simple Life. It was she who first urged me to publish these writings and who named the book. Some months back I went to her with a thought. Many of the readers of this book would be setting out on seemingly unfamiliar territory. I told her I would like to somehow match the risk that the reader was taking, so that there might be more commonness between us. We decided to commit ourselves to illustrating the book with photographs. Neither of us had much experience. We took an old miniature camera that I had obtained a number of years ago but had seldom used. It seemed to be an adequate piece of equipment. We decided that the subject matter of our photographs should be ordinary things that we frequently pass by each day. We would try to learn from our camera the same lessons that the reader would be learning from the words of the book. We would look for our subjects only in our own backyard or along the way in the various journeys we take each year to other communities. The process has been a spiritually rewarding one.

There is nothing more to say. What follows will speak for itself.

BROTHER TOLBERT McCARROLL

STARCROSS
Annapolis, California

I

THE STORY

You are a necessary part of a long story. Your parents and grandparents should have helped you feel your place in the story when you were yet a young child. But awhile back it seemed as if everyone forgot the story. So you grew up wondering about your value and your worth. You have searched for a place where you can belong. Now, when you are older and it is harder, you must learn that your value is in being you and you belong here.

Learn from a flower. Many ages ago a seed became a flower. That flower produced seeds. The seeds grew into flowers. Each flower you look at today is part of a solid line of existence going back to the beginning of life. Each flower needs every flower and seed that has gone before it.

You are a flower and a seed. You are part of a story which began with the first cell of life. That story will continue on after you. The many people and things you have touched in your life will be influenced by you. The history of the world would not be the same if you had not been here. The small ripples you cause today may bring huge waves in ages to come.

It is wrong for you to go moping about. It is wasteful to be dissipating your energy on frivolous activities. It is sad for you to be grasping at tinsel and building flimsy nests.

You are a guardian of the seeds for the world to come. All that has gone before and all that is yet to come is within you. Through you passes mankind's saving fire. You are running in a relay. This is the moment you have been chosen to hold the torch.

You cannot refuse to run. Whatever you do is part of your page in the story of life.

Be yourself. That is who you were meant to be. You are a note, a necessary note in a beautiful song!

II

SEASONS

A tree knows where it is on nature's wheel. Whatever the position—budding, in full leaf, with ripe fruit—it is all part of being a tree.

There are seasons in your life. Do not try to escape a season. If you try to bear fruit when it is time to bud, you may never bud.

Listen to the song of nature. Every year is a cycle. There is a time for activity and a time for quiet. There are moments of beginning and moments of ending. There are seasons for moving and seasons for renewal. Be still and learn. See nature's story unfold. Watch a bird and a tree. Learn about the commonness between you and the bird. Let the tree help you find your place.

Be aware of the day. There are seasons to a day. The dawn is the spring. Summer is at midday. The afternoon is autumn. Winter comes at night. You were made to experience this cycle each day. Remove your walls of protection. Move in rhythm with the day. Always remember that tomorrow there is another cycle, another turn of the wheel.

Every breath is a cycle of life. Take in the sweet spring of your breath. Fill up your lungs with the summer of the cycle. Experience the autumn joy of letting go. Be empty and still in the winter of your breath. Now breathe again, for there is always a new beginning and a new ending.

You will never take a breath more or less important than the one you are taking now. You will never be in a day or year more or less important than the one you are in now.

Every single moment is a new beginning for all life. This present second could see the end of all. This instant is a new beginning for all. If you really jump into a now-moment you will be completely renewed.

Life, like an ocean, is made up of many waves. There are waves for each moment, each day, each year, each life. If you hunger after a sense of completeness, be in harmony with the waves.

III

GOD

When you are small everyone bigger than you is a god. They have power. You learn that gods are to be placated.

When you are big enough to be god to someone else you are shown the mask of God. You are told stories about the goodness and justice of God.

When you are tall enough to see into the eyes of the mask you discover that people no bigger than you are wearing the mask. They have used the mask so you would listen to things they wanted to say to you. You are angry. You turn away from the mask.

This could be the end of your relationship with the concept of God. If you are fortunate you will run across some truly spiritual people. If you believe that they have no desire to determine your path or control your behavior you will feel free to listen to their experiences.

First, you hear that the God mask is a picture painted for those who are not participating in the Divine Experience. There may be some sadness. Down deep all of us wish for a father who will get us out of trouble—one who constantly thinks of us. But flowing with the sadness comes a realization of inner strength.

Then you will hear that there is a source for this picture of God. Some call it the God-head, or the Tao, or the Divine Darkness. There is a rhythm in all of life. The rhythm can only be heard in moments of quiet. If you are in harmony with this rhythm there will be a sense of completeness in you and in all the people and things you touch. At first you look outside yourself for the rhythm and you only hear a faint sound. Then you listen inside.

When you hear the song you must decide what you will do. You can wander in search of other tunes. You can stand rigid and continue to listen. Or, you can let the song possess you. You can become a part of the rhythm of life. Then you will have been found by the God-head.

IV

PRAYER

When you guide a child you help him develop his strength. You teach him not to ask you to solve a problem that he could face himself. The spoiled child does not want there to be any problems. If there is an adult who caters to him the child never develops his strength and goes through life holding tight to his mediocre images of existence.

So it is with prayer. If you ask for favors you make prayer a cold, mechanical process. Some sit in quiet meditation in order to have joy or peacefulness. Others pray that they may have a wish fulfilled or be assured a place among the elite of heaven or earth. Such people are blinded by the mask of self.

The Indian girl who rises with the sun does not do so because she wants something. She silently faces the east because she is part of the process of life that brings the sun. In the quiet she listens to the song of the dawn and lets it awaken a song within her.

Prayer is a touching. Move to the quiet within you. Let no thought or desire possess you. Stay within your inner stillness as if you were waiting at home for a great guest. You must learn patience. Be sure you are in when the guest comes. You will feel a gentle soft touch. When you do, then reach out and touch that which is touching you. Gently take your guide's hand and be led deep into the waters of solitude. You will leave behind all games, all desires, all greed, all dullness. Finally, you will leave you behind.

When you exit from your prayer you can travel

back over the same old road and pick up all the armor you cast aside. But many other doors are also open to you. You can awake to a new life. The moment of touching is a moment of death and rebirth. All that is you can be recreated in that moment.

Prayer is a new dawn.

V

LISTENING

In every corner of your world there blows a gentle wind that sings a silent song. You must listen for that song.

Usually your mind is filled with questions, arguments and expectations. Do not add more by considering how you will go about listening or congratulating yourself on how well you are doing. And especially do not believe that you know what you are going to hear. It is enough that you know the beginning. If you try to guess what will follow you will not hear what you were meant to hear. So, you must listen without expectations. Indeed, you must not expect that you will hear anything at all. For there is no object or goal to your listening. You are not listening for something. The listening itself is the end of the journey. Do not climb a mountain in order to listen. Go down into the valley.

Listening is emptying out. It means giving up everything. Remove your inner noise and the silent song will enter in. The song is being sung all the time. The breeze that bears this song comes from deep stillness. It is its nature to enter into any silence it encounters. You do not have to capture the song. It is not possible for you to do so. If you would experience the song you must be silent and listen to the stillness at your core.

Men and women do not hear what is constantly being spoken to them. Even those who profess to be longing for the song often make so much noise in their quest that there is no room for the song to enter in.

All that is required of you is that you learn to be truly quiet. Do that and all else will happen without your effort. The willow has only to stand still and the wind will move its branches. If the willow tried to create a wind by frantically waving its branches it would miss the real wind when it came. The attempt to create a wind will quickly exhaust you. When the wind of the silent song touches you, you are refreshed. So, like the willow, stand still.

All your life your heart has been singing a little soundless song. Listen to the song of your heart, because it is part of the great silent song. Open the door of your heart and the wind of the Spirit will come like an arrow to a target. Simply uncover the target and wait for what you cannot hear or see. The arrow knows what to do. That is all that is necessary.

VI

GROWTH

Growth is another word for living. When you stop growing you begin to die. Growth is spiritual youth and vitality. If you have unfolded today, if you are different from yesterday, then you are younger than yesterday.

Spiritual growth means discarding unnecessary things. When you are born you already have all you need. Furthermore, you are given all that you will ever get. You are just like a seed. All that you require is contained within you at birth, but for various reasons you clutter up your inner space and still you shout, "I want more." And the more you add the more you want. Discover the process of getting rid of what you have. Learn the joy of having less.

Many people do not grow because they are not themselves. You must begin by being yourself, no matter what that means. If you are self-centered and lazy, do not try to look like or be anything else. And then the process of growth can begin.

When some people discover who they are they become fascinated and never move. They are hypnotized by the image they see in the mirror. Slowly they sink into the mire, looking only at the mirror they hold before their face. Those who choose to change put down the mirror and move toward a spiritual conversion.

The gateway to the spiritual path is you. Look inside if you want to find the wisdom to grow. Everything you need is waiting for you. As you truly become yourself you become less conscious of yourself. You simply are who you are. All of the great conversions in history have meant simply a person discovering his own nature. Behind the self-centered brat is a divine flame. It may take many years for the flame to be liberated, but it is there. No matter how hard it is to accept you must understand that the only difference between you and any religious person you admire is that your hero has discovered his own nature.

Many may die without knowing about this treasure within them. Most discover it only a few hours or days before their last breath. Some do it much earlier.

VII

AWAKE

You just passed by what you are looking for and it is not there any longer.

The trouble is you do not know when you are asleep. In the days when people took spirituality more seriously a student would look for a master with whom to live. He focused his whole attention on this quest. He found a master and would be accepted as a student. Year after year he would follow his master around. He waited. Nothing would happen. Finally, after many years he would realize there was nothing to wait for. All this time he was being offered instruction but he did not see it.

Spiritual riches are always wrapped in plain paper and when you open the box it is empty.

It is important that you become self-affirming, that you not look to the opinions of others to find value. It is only self-affirming people who can feel the spiritual significance of a particular situation. Two people can enter the same spiritual house. The one sees only classes to attend, rules to discover, some dishes to wash, some times to be quiet. He is patient. He waits. Everything is ordinary. Finally, he is bored and leaves. The environment is not at all like his fantasy of a spiritual life.

The other student does not look outside but listens inside. Her own inner voice translates for her the songs of the house. For her this is the beginning of the most exciting adventure that life can offer. She sees many magnificent happenings around her. She understands that all these wonderful things are just an ordinary part of life.

Impatiently you find a guide. And with even more impatience you follow him around waiting for him to get down to the really important things. There may come a moment when you discard your expectations. Then you will slowly look around and utter a loud—Oh!

Then, your guide will smile.

VIII

TEACHERS

There will be times when you will use a spiritual guide. Your attitude will limit your teacher's ability to help you. He can only talk to you about the things you are ready to hear.

You will often be disappointed in him. You have gone in search of a great spiritual master and all you find is a rather mundane and very human person. Soon you realize that he is no better than you! The person who seems to be ready to ascend to the heights of heaven is not a teacher but an actor. He will help you live in a spiritual daydream in exchange for a little idolatry. The true teacher will not attempt to encounter you except where you are. He will often appear a little foolish. If underneath your mask you are babbling on, then your teacher will babble. As he walks along on your path he will try to point out a few things that will help you slow down a little, but he can only talk about what interests you.

Have you ever attempted to put a toddler into a stroller? She does not want to sit down, she wants to get over there. How can you get over there by sitting down? How do sitting and moving go together? She knows what is good for her. After a while she may decide that you may have a feasible plan but she does not want to be the one to try it. Could she not just watch the stroller roll down by itself or why do you not get in it and show her how it works? Perhaps she watches another little child in a stroller and gets the idea. Now she knows how to do it better than you so she gets in backwards. You have to take her out and turn her around. And she yells—what does taking her out of the stroller have to do with getting her into the stroller? About this time she decides to become an expert on the right rear wheel. She plays with it and fixes her attention totally upon it. After all, is not this the really important part of the stroller? Then, just as you get her in, she decides that it has taken too long, or you do not know what you are doing, or she is not able to do it, or it will not work, so she demands to get out and go back into the house.

Getting a child into a stroller is much simpler than guiding a person onto a spiritual path. You look to your teacher to show you how to be fulfilled. Yet the only thing your teacher has to give you is a little advice about not seeking fulfillment, or power, or love, or respect, or anything else. It is as if you had come to a beautiful walled city. If you attempt to write your own ticket and decide what is best for you all that your teacher can do is walk around the outer wall with you. So long as you have desires or expectations you make your teacher walk in a circle. Give up your desires and he can quickly take you inside the wall.

A teacher is only a mirror. He helps you see yourself. He is a medium for the true guide residing within you. The teacher gives your inner guide a voice. And when you and this ever-present guide engage in a flowing conversation your teacher will quietly leave. Then if you want to find your teacher you must look on his path. There the teacher will be walking and talking to the guide within him.

IX

CONTROL

Turn on the heat and you kill the cold. Switch on the light and you destroy the darkness. Manipulate the conversation and you will never hear the words that were about to come.

You have no right to control anything that is not you. Controlling other things, animals, people, ideas, is what makes you separate and lonely. When you see all life's inconveniences as your enemies, then you are setting yourself apart.

If you hear that a person a thousand miles away is having to spend an hour doing some work he does not enjoy you are not too concerned. But when you are that person you act as if the world were ending. You are not listening to the lessons around you. Instead you shout about the injustice, look for shortcuts, and start pushing the world around in order to gain an advantage. Try to look upon yourself as if you were a thousand miles away.

Your ancestors moved with the day. They rose when the sun came up. If one place became crowded they moved away. When it was dark they looked at the stars and then they slept. You protect yourself with a house and a blanket. You stay up late so that you need an alarm to control your sleep. You turn on the heater because it is cold or let a fan blow away the heat. You are like a nearsighted child running through a schoolhouse full of exciting activities, shutting all the doors. You are missing many lessons with your control.

You are so afraid that you will be deprived of

something that you reject your birthright without knowing what it is.

Be aware of all the hundreds of ways in which you are controlling and manipulating during the course of each day. Hesitate a moment each time you are tempted. Awareness is the beginning of growth.

Sometimes your ancestors destroyed life. They would kill an animal or a plant. They did so with respect. The animal was not an object or an enemy. The animal and the people were one. Only when you understand that you are one with all things can you safely destroy anything. The cold is not your enemy. You and the cold are one. You and the darkness are one. When you feel this, then you will move with grace, and with a smile, to do what it is right to do.

X

PEACE

You long for peace, yet there is no such thing as peace. It is nothing. Peace is simply the absence of troubles and worries. Troubles and worries are your attempts to control your future. You are given a chair to sit in, but instead you break it up for firewood in case you should get cold, or you use it for a torch to help you look around a corner. Forget the future. It is only a dream. Sit in the chair. Find your rest. If you forget the future you will have no trouble with this moment—this now. Anything that disturbs you is in the future. Sit down and there is no trouble now—or now—or now—or now. Make your life a series of nows. That is how you were meant to live.

Do not make a goal of inner peace. Peace is the absence of war, the cessation of hostilities, the end of striving. You go spinning around, fighting with yourself, with others, or with life itself. If you stop the fight you will find peace. Peace is not something to achieve. You cannot fight your way to it; it is something you do. You always have a choice: to fight or to be at peace.

You stop the fight when you stop acting as if you are different than you are and stop your longing after what others have. You try to be someone else because you do not think you have the strength to be yourself. But you do.

Being yourself means being old when you are young, and young when you are old. It means not looking at the peak when you start to climb the mountain. Being yourself means trusting in your ability and using all the strength you have. Being yourself means not dissipating your energy on petty things. When there is striving, cleverness and wanting, there is no peace.

You are like a dirty infant who is playing in the mud. You are angry because a bird will not do what you say. You are obsessed with the desire to have as much mud as another little child. You wallow around getting dirtier all the time. Yet, you are a royal child. You have everything you need for the adventure of life.

Come now. Wash your face. Walk out into the garden. Sit here in your chair. Rest. Be still. While you have been in the mud, the tree and the wind have been dancing together. Look at them. How beautifully they move together. No matter what happens to them, all will be well. For they are being themselves. They are not acting like things they are not. Neither are they denying what they are. You are a wind to a tree, and a tree to a wind. Be yourself. Do not live beneath your nature and all will be well with you.

XI

DETACHMENT

You like to look at red leaves in the fall. This is good; it increases your awareness and perhaps is even the beginning of the realization that the red leaves and you are one. But if you must see the red leaves—if you push someone aside in order to see the leaves—if you can think of nothing but the leaves—if you look at a person and think, "Here is someone who can drive me into the countryside to see more red leaves," then you are being possessed by your desire for red leaves. You are afraid you will miss something. You do not have something that you want. You are grasping. If you are to find your true nature and to follow the spiritual path you must learn to detach.

In the beginning the process of detachment seems cold. When a person sits in meditation or prays by resting in the Spirit she empties herself of everything. How lonely that sounds. But being alone is not necessarily lonely. To detach from your preoccupations is to have faith in the life process and to know that you are a part of it. Through detachment you do not forsake people and your environment. Detachment is a means of connecting with them at a deeper level. For it is not people or things that distract you, but your desires. It is from these desires that you must learn to detach.

Desires are like demons. There are many demons, each with his own name and characteristics. Some are called respectability, security, superiority, control, recognition, stubbornness; all creatures from the hell of Self. These are the demons that separate you from people and life. Suppose you look at a person and you feel competitive. Then you are not in contact with that person. If you can learn to detach from your competitive desires then you can begin to touch that person. If you see another person simply as an audience for your words or actions then you are trying to relate to that person on the level of the demons. You do not see the person at all, but simply yourself. If you detach from self you are free to see the other person and perhaps even to love that person.

Detachment begins by entering into the silence of your own inner being. The demons exist on the periphery of your inner world. Yet you seldom go past them to experience what lies at the center. Do not let the demons possess you. Push past them. Do not try to conquer them. Just detach from them. Move on. The greatest possible distraction is trying to push other distractions away. Let your thoughts and feelings dance and yell. Just move on. Sometimes you act as if you are your troubles. You are not your troubles. They are a part of you but not all of you. Move through them.

Do not make the mistake of cursing the demons or your troubles. They are valuable to you. Solving problems is not really important. Finding your true nature is of great importance. Unless you become who you are you will wander through life on a a barren and dusty road. Demons and troubles create a darkness. In this darkness you can find your inner light. You would not be able to find the flame of a candle on a desert at high noon. You can see the candle flame easily at midnight.

So do not despise the dog that barks during your meditation. If a thoughtless person has upset you do not blame him for your agitation at times of prayer. Remember it is you who chooses to plague yourself with the demons rather than continuing on your way. Look for your light. Nothing else matters.

XII

PAIN

The parents of all life are the sky and the earth. They come together to form a womb. Here all people, animals and plants receive what they need to travel their paths.

Storms accompany all bornings. It is in the wild turbulence that we learn the skills for our growth.

As you travel along your path there must be many springs. Without the cold and barren winter there can be no spring beauty. Winter is the season of the womb. Its pain is our friend, our beacon. It points out the direction for our journey. There are only two roads in life, growing and dying. The bud must go through the discomfort of unfolding or it will shrivel.

If we use our cleverness to avoid pain we will not learn valuable lessons. Bodily discomfort tells us when we have broken nature's rhythm. The pain in the heart reminds us of the winter of the womb, and again we can prepare for a new step in life.

You must not remain in the pain. It is only the vestibule of change. Suppose that on a hot August afternoon you come upon a cool lake. You can make two good choices. You can suffer the discomfort and insecurity of jumping in the lake. Or you can move away and come back to the lake another day. If you choose to remain fixed on the edge you will destroy yourself. There is no way of avoiding the shock of the plunge. No matter how clever you are the decision will always be the same—leap or turn away. If you will not make the choice your strength will fade away. Most of your sorrow in life comes from trying not to choose or from taking a half step.

Life is like a ladder. You climb up to a rung. Then you regain your composure. In time you become comfortable on the rung. Perhaps you even become an expert concerning this rung. You do not want to become a struggling beginner again. Yet, if you learn that each step is only a rung, you will welcome the freshness of each beginning. Then every step you take in life, even death itself, becomes an act of renewal.

XIII

FEAR

You are the only thief you need to fear. Other people can take things away from you, but only you can steal your own strength and peace. Only you can hold on to all the extra baggage that is weighing you down. You fear losing the very things that are draining your vitality.

There are two voices within you. One says that you must have insurance. "Bad times are coming and you cannot take care of yourself. Unless you have some advantage you will be trampled underfoot. So find some power and security. Get more money, prestige and titles." With all this you make a mask and hide behind it because you believe you are weak and inadequate.

There is also within you a quieter voice. If you are still you can hear this other voice. "You are strong, you already have enough—indeed you have too much. You have become a walking junkyard of unnecessary activities, things, ideas and strivings. You believe all these things benefit you by protecting you. In fact, they smother you. Get rid of your protections. Stand naked. Learn again that you were born with all you need, that you are a part of the flow of life!"

If you stop worrying about the past and planning for the future you will be able to experience the present now-moment. Only when you are truly in the now can you hear your rhythm and dance with it. Think of the petal on a daisy. It has no extra coat for a cold night, no umbrella for a hot day. Such protections would weigh the daisy down and eventually bend it away from the rest of the flower. Then there would be loneliness and feelings of being different and inadequate. It would do no good to add more overcoats and umbrellas; the extra weight would only make the problem worse.

Shedding your protections is uncomfortable. You will feel exposed when you drop your baggage. You will be tempted to save a little something—just in case! Do not do it.

Stand alone in the desert. You will begin again to see what is around you, to feel your strength. You will learn that you are at home.

XIV

TROUBLE

Do not play with your troubles or struggle with them. Go through them.

There is only one true trouble, your self-centeredness. Even when you are thinking of all your faults and inadequacies you do it fondly and with much attention. If you were not so concerned about how circumstances could bruise your delicate self you would experience no fear. You try to protect that which you were meant to discard. If you can become self-free then death itself is no threat, for what do you lose?

The most painful troubles are not outside events but inside gnawings. First, there is wanting to fill up to the brim. Then comes the hunger to have your feelings stroked and to get so lost in your passions that everyone becomes an object. Only one thing will matter, will this person help or hinder your being stroked? Then, there is the desire to hold on to whatever you think you have. Next is the belief that it is easier to control situations, people, and even the future than it is to develop trust in yourself and in the' life force. Then, there is the temptation to wallow in sadness for not getting things your own way. Then comes the wish to improve your distress by finding an object upon whom you can angrily dump your inner tensions and vital force. Following close behind is the lazy longing to be free of the present moment and to drift aimlessly. Then, there is the opportunity to conceal yourself behind a mask and to strive to look good in the eyes of the universe. Finally, there are moments when it would feel good to deceive yourself into believing in the mask. If you do this, then you will begin to protect your specialness with walls of arrogance, and your separation from life will be complete. But this lonely course is not the only one open to you.

These inner troubles are not overpowering situations; these are only wandering wild creatures. They will always be knocking at your door, as they have continually knocked at the door of every man and woman in the story of life. If you recognize the knock do not answer it. If you do open the door, do not receive them as guests; do not give them house room. Close the door and go about your business. You will be stronger for the experience.

Should you meet these creatures on the street, you will be more vulnerable. Not because they are more powerful, but because you will be more tempted to fight them. Do not struggle with these creatures. You will always lose, for the fight itself takes you away from the vital task of living and your strength slowly fades. Simply go through these creatures. Let them continue their squabbling. You can always walk through them if you have someplace to go. Plunge yourself fully into the business of living in this now-moment. Then, like a leaf on the river, you will be carried past the menacing animals on the shore. You are of the river; they are of the shore.

If by chance you forget and start fighting with them, disengage as quickly as you can. Never mind your wounds; they will heal. Just get out of that pit and back on the path. If you want some instant relief, let the creatures fight each other. If you are sorely attacked by your desire to hoard your feelings and possessions, let that creature face your desire to appear to the world as a spiritually advanced and generous person. As those two struggle with each other their hold on you will lessen. Then quickly make your exit.

You are a warrior. But these pitiful little creatures are not your adversaries. Let them come. Develop your strength by moving through them. Leave them behind in the murky shadows. Step out into the light and continue down your path.

XV

STRUGGLES

You were born with some weaknesses; you picked up others in the first months and years of your life.

Much of your life has been spent attempting to get rid of these natural weaknesses or lamenting over them. "If only I did not want to be recognized." "If only I did not want to look good." "If only I were not so stubborn." "If only I were not so lazy." "If only" is a waste of time. Trying to rid yourself of your weak impulses is futile.

The impulse to indulge your weakness always presents an opportunity for growth. There should be no shame or remorse in being tempted, for it is because of your weak tendencies that you are able to develop your strength.

You are like the blade of a knife. When you were born your edge was sharp. But it did not stay sharp. With use it will dull and need to be resharpened. So at birth you were also given a whetstone. Your natural weakness is your whetstone. Through it you sharpen your edge. Without it you would remain dull.

Your weakness seldom comes forward when you are truly sharp and vital. It is not needed. But you cannot be that way all the time. You are supposed to use your sharpness and little by little, you lose that perfect keenness. Then your whetstone appears—a tempting inclination to indulge yourself. Do not contemplate or talk about what to do. Do it. Throw yourself into it completely. If you want more of something, go the other way. If you want more wine, drink water. Rain does not fall unless there are clouds in the sky. If you wish to avoid getting wet you must act when the first little cloud appears. Move quickly and you will not only avoid the storm but also regain your sharpness. Welcome the struggle. Your greatest treasure lies buried inside your greatest fault.

Use the fault and find the treasure.

XVI

DEATH

Dying is not separate from living. You will die as you have lived. If you have been self-centered in life then when you are dying you will focus on what you are losing. If you have felt yourself to be a part of a story and learned to let go of your distractions and desires, then your dying will be a time of strength, honesty, sharpness, and most of all a time of completeness.

We know little about dying. We know nothing about death. Some insects lay their eggs in October and then die. The eggs hatch in June. There is half of the year that is completely unknown to these small creatures, but it does not matter. They live their lives completely. They do not have to know anything else. You would not go to a corpse and ask for advice on living. So do not go to a living person and ask questions about death. It is the business of a dead person to be dead and of a living person to be alive.

When you are born, begin to live. When you bud, bud. When you eat, eat. When you flower, flower. When you sleep, sleep. When you listen, listen. When you die, die. Dying is simply another moment in life.

Your life can prepare you for dying. Your death can assist you in life. Death is not the enemy. The full realization that you will some day die can sharpen your awareness of what it means to live. You often act as if you were immortal when you become involved with petty, selfish things. If you accept the fact that you will die, it will help you disengage from these entanglements and focus on the process of living.

Be still for a moment. Inside you is an image of your last moments of life. Experience that image. Let this image teach you something about your response to now—to this present moment.

Death is a name we give the act of returning. It is only your individuality which will really die. Watch a sunflower grow and bloom and bear fruit. See the great stalk wither, turn brown and fall to the ground. You say that it is dead. But nothing in nature can really cease to exist. A number of elements were brought out of their quiet to produce what you have labeled "sunflower." The plant performs its mission. Now it returns to its source. As it does so it nourishes other parts of the great community of life. What remains of the sunflower becomes quiet and after awhile merges with the ground again. Perhaps it will remain in the quiet forever or it may again be used for another of life's stories.

You are like a drop of rain. There is beauty and joy in being a single drop. It is exciting to fall. You reflect beautifully all the colors of the rainbow. And, there is also weariness in being so individual and fragile and in having to contend with time and space.

There will come a time when like a rain drop you will lose your separateness and merge into a pool of water. All that is you has come into a great stillness. Nothing of you is lost. You are now part of life's force.

Soon the pool will merge with the earth and once again there is the strength of complete stillness.

XVII

HOPE

You are an instrument through whom can pass the wind of the life-Spirit. You cannot light a spark within another person. Neither can you ever take credit for what another person does, nor blame for what that person does not do. You can only seek satisfaction from the way that you protect and feed the spark within you.

Sometimes the wind moves through you in a way in which your song is helpful to another. But without your own song you can never give nor receive.

When you do not trust that you are truly a part of the scheme of life you try to look ahead. You strive for security and certainty. You will never see the whole picture. Therefore you can never be completely secure.

Despair comes from trying to control matters over which you have no power. Hope comes from taking responsibility for yourself.

If you cannot find security by your grasping then you look around for others to blame for your discomfort. All these actions build walls within you and the wind of the Spirit cannot move through you. Your strings remain limp. There is no song.

You add more walls until you have built a solid prison for yourself. Now you are truly enslaved. You hate the jailer but you cannot see his face. This could be the end. It could be the beginning. Remember that every prison has a chapel. Travel through the corridors of your own dark stillness until you come to a little room. Inside that room is a tiny spark that never goes out. If you blow on the spark with your full attention you will be able to make a flame. Then light a torch. Examine the walls. See how fragile they are. Find the jailer. Look on his face. You are the jailer.

If you prefer to live in a prison you will extinguish your torch and return to the darkness.

But, if there is within you a nostalgia for freedom you will hold your torch high. You will not allow yourself to be dominated by desires to have and to control. You will not let yourself be possessed by things and thoughts. Then you will stand and watch the walls of your prison melt away like clay in the rain.

XVIII

VIRTUE

It does not matter what ideas you develop or even what actions you take.

A clump of cut weeds traveling before a high wind makes many motions similar to a tree swaying in the breeze. The difference is that one is rooted and at home, and the other is wandering wildly in foreign lands.

It is your roots that will keep you from becoming an erudite spiritual dilettante worshipping at the altar of self-love. These roots are developed by surrendering to your spiritual path. The name for the roots is "virtue."

Virtue is the muscle tone that develops from the daily and hourly training of a spiritual warrior. Virtue is not a prissy morality. It is the presence of an inner strength that results from living a disciplined and aware life which emphasizes a detachment from self-centered desire. Be always alert and vital; there can never be any time off. A fish cannot live out of water and you cannot long continue without your daily discipline.

Like the warrior and the athlete focus your full attention on the present now-moment. Do not hold on to things that have already happened, nor grasp for things yet to come. Do not waste your time on guilt or regret. If you have gone too far to the right swing to the left and keep on running. Let your responses be quick, sharp and without reserve. Do not entertain that which is shadowy. Value only what you can rely upon.

There are no accidents in your life; nothing happens by chance. Eat a lot and you get fat. Each step of the process may not be easily observable but there is no mystery about it. If misfortune is a frequent visitor, look for the lesson in the pain. Detach from your desire to have things go your own way. Suffering is like a rope around a person who has wandered off a mountain trail. It keeps him from falling off the cliff. Do not fight the pain; learn from it. Find your way back to the path; correct your steps.

Virtue is not just an individual matter. It is important to return good for evil. The whole world is the house in which you live. If you find a mess on the floor, clean it up, or you will have to live in it. Justice is not a spiritual consideration. If you are on a boat and all the passengers move to one side, the boat will capsize. If you try to determine who is at fault, who should go to the other side, it will be too late to stop the boat from tipping over. Quickly put your weight on the other side. If you are the target of someone's hateful attack, or if you see such an ,attack directed toward another, immediately try to release your natural gentleness by selfless acts of compassion. When you see a friend step from his path for the sake of gaining something look to see how you can be more frugal in your own wants and more generous toward others. If you see a child across the street carelessly uproot some plants restore the balance by giving extra care that day to helping things grow. If the desire for power leads people to kill each other in a distant land be particularly aware of how you can nourish your community by not taking precedence over others.

Do not attempt to make a virtue out of virtue, for that is simply self-love. If you take pride in your poverty it is more burdensome to your spiritual growth than the wealth you rejected. Let your assistance to others be secret and automatic. The desire for recognition robs you of virtue and increases your belief in your separateness. Have no ulterior purposes for your actions. Act quickly and spontaneously, and you will not be conscious of your action or your virtue.

XIX

ANGER

As you walk the spiritual path the cold flame of anger must not burn long in your breast.

Most of your anger comes from being artificial and indirect. When you do not speak or act in complete honesty, or when you make a little compromise for politeness' sake, you plant the seed of anger. If a person tries to involve you in a clever conversation you must be guided by your inner light. If you are uncomfortable you must say so. If you play the game, you have put a cancer in your spirit which will spread and grow all by itself. In time your anger will reach the bursting point and you will pour out the venom upon others or harbor it within yourself until it eats up your body and soul. When someone hands you poison you must not hold it even for a moment.

If you are angry do not act as if you are not. There is no disgrace in having anger—only in hiding it. If there is anger in you let it out as soon as you know of its presence. Express your anger. Let your outer actions be the same as your inner feelings. This is the only honest route.

Sadder than the person who tries to deny his anger is the person who enjoys it. For some the Self is so big it hides the whole world. Such a person is angry because he is not given what he wants, yet he will not tell anyone what he wants. At times he does not even try to find out for himself. This person is a coward whose only pleasure is in punishing the world.

Strive to be always open and honest and to be

incapable of anger. Should some poison sneak by and fester in your heart throw it out as soon as you discover it. Learn from the experience and be more careful next time.

Gradually the force that was used in your anger will be directed along other lines. The violent state of anger will be replaced by inner peace. It takes a long time. Be patient. Be honest. Go one step at a time. Never step backwards.

XX

JUDGING

When you judge another person's conduct you attempt to exile the accused from the human family. You have no right to do that. When you judge another it is you who will be punished. As you indulge your anger and scorn you slowly become separated from your brothers and sisters, and you will walk a lonely path.

In order to keep from judging another five things are necessary. First, express your true feelings promptly, and resentment will not build up within you. Second, do not blame others for your difficulties, for only you can stand in your own way. Third, practice detachment, and do not let your environment or the conduct of others possess you. Fourth, strive to be aware of people as people. Your fellow humans are not machines to be evaluated according to how they function. Fifth, each day spend a little time searching for your commonness with others.

From time to time, people will trick you, outsmart you, or even visit evil and harm upon you. Do not poison yourself with judgments or harbor resentments. Try to feel some pity for these people. The person who is clever in relationships with others lives a hollow life. Those who always get their own way usually lose their way. People who must be in control of everything never relax. They must watch out for the best advantage every moment, for if they do not someone will deprive them of something. You may be irritated with the child who steals everyone else's candy, but you do not envy him his stomachache. Those who win, lose. Suppose a piece of grass could raise itself above its fellow blades and stretch itself out on top of them in the sun. How good it feels. But this piece of grass is now separated from the many tiny and almost invisible roots that connected it to the ground and brought it nourishment. Soon it will wither and die.

You judge others because you judge yourself. Since you judge yourself you assume others are also judging you. So you point to another to divert attention away from you. Learn not to judge yourself, and it will not occur to you to judge another.

No one can take anything of real value from you. Judging another is simply self-indulgence, for it is easier for you to judge another's path than to walk on your own.

Do not judge yourself for judging. Let the past take care of itself. Jump into the present. Do not try to live in yesterday's wave. There is a wave beneath you now. It is ready to carry you away on the voyage of life. Ride the wave you are on and forget the others.

XXI

LOVE

There is love within you. You long to make a joyful connection with every flower and animal around you. You also have love for people in your heart. This love will turn into a hard lump unless you let it out.

When you want love it is not love. Rather it is a desire for being stroked, comforted or pampered. Neither is love something you give. That is an impersonal fantasy of a relationship that exists only in your head. Love is something you do. It is an act. It is a genuine touching, which leaves you vulnerable and traveling in uncertain territory.

Love is a two-way thing. You cannot love a flower unless you let the flower love you. Love is a mutual touching.

There is also within you a homesickness calling you to the love of stillness. Do not go traveling abroad to find what has remained at home. When you love you move to meet that which is moving to meet you. The stillness within you is reaching out to you.

If you would release the love within you two things are necessary:

You must stop your busyness, for the busy man is only interested in his busyness. Love is a jealous mistress who will not stay in the same place with lesser suitors.

Also, you must not have anything that anyone can steal from you. If other beings can deny or deprive you of things you value then you will not love them. If you believe you need particular people and that your happiness is dependent on them then you cannot love them.

When you truly love you are not conscious of loving. Love all of life in the way your finger loves your hand. And, when you are simple and free of selfish desires, your heart will open naturally, like the petals of a flower.

XXII

THOU

There are times when you will lose your way. At those times you will wander lost and lonely. Each step takes you farther away from your path. Frantically you will thrash around in the wilderness. One thought possesses you. How can you stop the dull, constant heartache.

After a while you may give up. You play a game with yourself. You change your opinion of what is important. You try to forget the path. You go seeking money, respect, knowledge, power, or some other distinction. You will achieve your goal and stand out from the crowd. The more distinctions you have the more separate you feel. You are alone and lonely.

You look at people according to how they function. Can this man drive me across town? Will this woman assist me? Is this the right teacher to impart knowledge to me? If I am in a relationship with this person will I feel loving and warm?

You may feel guilty about looking at other people with an eye toward what is in it for you. If so, do not try to correct this situation by talking a great deal about love. Do not make love an obligation or a technical concept.

There are simpler ways to live. Stop trying to find a ladder that will reach the sky. Stay still and the sky will touch you. Feel the earth beneath you. All the plants and animals that touch the earth have a common bond. Every woman you pass is your sister, every man is your brother. You do not know the name or capacity of the person who stands before you. If you try to detach from any melodrama about the two of you coming together you may be able to see this fellow being. If you are not possessed with selfishness you may feel something deep within you. It is as if you are within that person and you have the same person within you. At that moment there is no separateness. It is as if you remembered a winter evening long ago when as little children you two sat gazing silently into the fire. At that moment there is no loneliness.

XXIII

HUMILITY

You believe you are special. You may have special gifts, or perhaps you have special problems. But there is some way in which you are different and deserving of special attention. Of course you have specific gifts and problems, but everyone has.

Humility is simply working to overcome your specialness. It is not asking others to do for you the things you can do for yourself. It is doing the little things. There is no way of stopping your preoccupation with yourself unless you give yourself something else with which to be occupied. There are many things you can do. Start by washing the ring out of the bathtub.

Humility is not an abstract thing. Neither is it a melodramatic self-abasement which you inflict on others. Humility is washing out the bathtub, making your own bed, getting your own tea. Stop the game of getting out of menial tasks. Bend. Do not expect others to wait on you. Go the other way. Do things for others.

It is much easier for you to go serve the lepers in the South Seas than to clean the ring out of the bathtub. When you serve the lepers you prove to yourself that you are special. When you wash the bathtub you learn that you have a common connection with every other person. No one is better than anyone else, and no one really believes that.

Search for your commonness and then you can have the freedom to be different. The cotton must become a thread before it can be dyed and woven into the tapestry. When you feel a commonness with others you will not feel competition. You will use your gifts simply because you have them and not to enlarge your ego. Then you will be in harmony with other gifts.

To be humble is to be like water. Water flows into low places. It is soft and yet can overcome the hardest stone. It is beautiful and is nothing special.

Be common. Be as common as the dawn sun on a winter day; as common as a field of flowers on a summer afternoon. To experience your commonness is to be rich. To feel your specialness is to be poor and lonely.

XXIV

YIELDING

You are always planning and organizing the future. When things go contrary to your master plan you stiffen and resist. Be careful. In a high wind only the pliant things will survive. The rigid tree will break off. The tree that yields to the storm never loses its connection with the ground which links it to all other forms of life.

When you must have your own way you rail against circumstances, people, or even life itself. You fight and manipulate, and probably eventually you will get your own way. Why then, is your happiness so short-lived; why the dull ache in your heart? You have used all of your strength and force to win. You have pounded away at what you think of as the problem. Your pounding has driven a wedge between you and all the other parts of life. You are victorious; you are now on top, special, separate, and spent.

To yield is not to avoid an onslaught or to cower before it; for that results in as much separateness as if you had won. To yield is to meet the onslaught; to realize that any pain comes from your own desires; to remove the wall of separateness between you and your troubles; to dance with the onslaught; to conserve your own energy; to open your arms and to use the power that is hurtling toward you.

Often when you stop protecting yourself you will find that your great problem was in reality a great opportunity. The usual price of admission to a new level of living is your self-will. If you stop writing your own ticket you may find there is one already waiting for you.

You do not know the song yet. You are only just beginning to hear some of the notes. Every time you strive to have your own way you bring discord into your life. Once you start striving there is no end to it. Others will strive with you. Nothing will go right. You will have no peace.

Hold fast to your own interior light. Then you can take all the exterior things in an even fashion. Know that sometimes things are hard and sometimes they are easy. Each rhythm and cycle has its purpose.

You spend much time in worrying about what to do, in deciding between this and that. Be more accepting of what is sent to you. Do not attempt to form life into your shape. Conform to your home, the earth. Then you will know your place, and your heart will be light.

XXV

CHOICE

No matter what thoughts come your way or what feelings you experience, you always have a choice. It is a gift you are given. There is permanently implanted within you a light that longs for its nature and yearns to shine. You can always choose to let this light cut through the darkness. Many things will come your way in the course of a day. You cannot control these events. They are the results of how and where you live. But you do have choices about how you react to these occurrences. Suppose someone carelessly misuses some property of yours. You can hold on to your irritation and punish that person by denouncing him, or dramatically forgive him. Or, you can punish the whole world by feeling sorry for yourself. There is another choice, and that is to accept the event as an event. Be aware of it, react to it, and then like any other distraction let it come and let it go. You always have the choice to take all things evenly, to hold on to nothing, to receive each irritation as if you had only fifteen minutes left to live.

The spider has no choice. She is a spider and every minute she must act and move and think like a spider. Her lack of choice is her freedom. For freedom means being yourself and moving into the space that fits you. Being so much yourself that you are not conscious of you.

Unlike the spider you do have a choice and your freedom lies in learning to use your choice. Give ink to a child and he may make a beautiful picture or he may dump it on the rug. You dump your gift of choice out on the rug when you use your choice to take a vacation from life. Taking it easy on yourself is making it hard for yourself, for you deny your strength and lose your self-respect. Even the simplest task is hard when you have an image of yourself as being weak.

Sometimes you choose to protect yourself and to stop the necessary training for becoming a full participant in the adventure of life. You insist on writing your own ticket. You know what you need. You know what is good for you. You abandon a difficult task because you have figured out that it is bad for your body or your psyche. You even have the choice to decide that you are psychologically sick and therefore unable to do anything except find someone to take responsibility for you. If you train yourself to believe you are a person who has strong uncontrollable desires that must be satiated you will put yourself upon a shelf.

When you misuse your gift of choice you gradually fade into the dull gray cloud that drifts in and out of life.

The only choice you do not have is to refuse to make a choice, for that itself is a choice to continue what you are doing. Often you use a stick to try to make a mud puddle come clear. One of your most frequent opportunities is to choose to stop using the stick and to let the mud settle.

At every moment of your life it is as if you are being pulled in two directions. One force seems to drag you downward toward the swamp and another seems to pull you upward toward the clear sky. If you remember that you always have a choice there is no problem. Suppose you are walking along a mountainous trail with a steep cliff dropping down to your left. Your left foot slips a bit. There is no problem unless you forget that your right foot is on solid ground.

Choose to remember the foot that is on solid ground. Choose to let your light shine. Choose not to be conscious of yourself. Soon you will discover that you are simply choosing to stay on your spiritual path and not to be sidetracked. This is choosing to live.

XXVI

FATIGUE

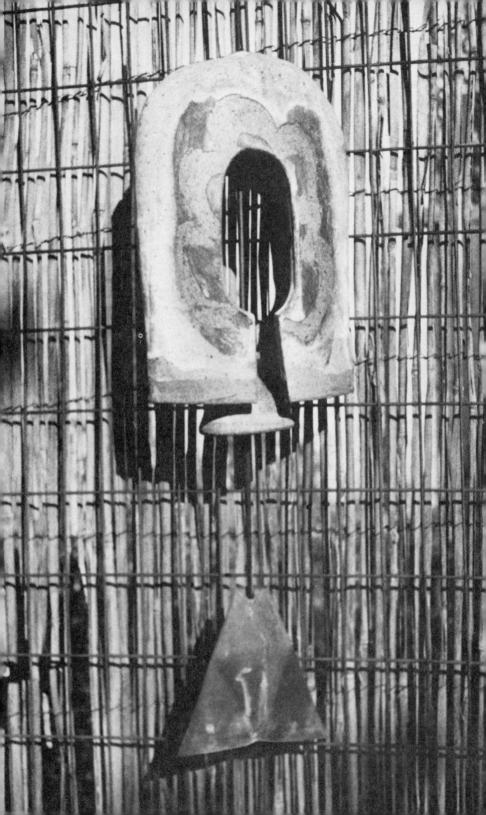

M uch of your life will be spent in recuperating. You are chronically ill as a result of being overweight. You have too many things hanging on you, too many desires inside of you. Frequently the weight of all your possessions and longings will press you down until you are too weak to do any-thing but go to bed. You have been·whizzing around so much that all your inner strength has been used up. For a while you slow down and you stop collect-ing things.

When you become still and peaceful your strength begins to build up again. As a little of your vitality returns you are convinced that you are healthy once more and you begin again all your attempts to gain things, and positions, and ideas, and people. You feel so much better that you think you must be well. Now you can again decide what is best for you, using the simple criterion of doing what you want to do. So once again your spiritual strength will be dis-sipated.

You are born with an inner force. When you re-lease this strength for external things, like gaining, mastering, competing, and possessing, it is quickly used up. When the force is left to develop in the quiet emptiness of your inner being it grows and grows. Leave the hot wax in the hollow at the top of the candle and it is fuel for the flame; spill the wax and it makes splotches that are difficult to remove.

At times of spiritual fatigue you are given the op-portunity to plug the holes through which your strength has spilled out. Then the light within you will gradually brighten. You must remain still and resist the temptation to return to your normal activities. Do not assume you know what is going on. Act as if any sense of well-being is an illusion, and then you will hear and feel the quiet pulse of your interior life. Focus only on this pulse until it has a strong and even rhythm. It may take hours, days, weeks or years.

Your spiritual sickness can be just an annoying interruption in your attempt to stuff yourself, or it can be a gift which will enable you to provide adequate fuel for the light within you.

XXVII

PLANTING

D o not try to reason out your life. Quietly walk along the silent paths of your inner garden. Eventually, you will enter a selfless moment where there is no time. You will feel at home, and one with all of life. Then listen, really listen. You will hear your destiny tinkling like a distant silver bell.

When you know the general direction of your path you must not wait for your destiny to be delivered to you. Worse still, you must not try to make it take place. You must plant.

If a good farmer feels within him a desire to raise corn he does not wait for someone to give him the corn crop. Neither does he take a handful of sand and try to form an ear of corn. The farmer plants a kernel of corn, and he devotes his attention to that piece of corn. As the kernel sprouts and grows the farmer learns from it what next to do.

Once you have heard your destiny go and find a seed to plant. If you will be a creator and builder then today make a loaf of bread—not tomorrow but today. Should you hear yourself drawn to a life with children then today go and touch a child. And, let a child touch you. When the bell within you sounds like a temple bell and you yearn for spiritual solitude realize that you are your own monastery. Today establish your monastic routine. Your contemplative regime can only begin in the bustle of the noisy city.

Plant your seed now. Let it grow. In a few days you will learn what to do next. You must never neglect your plant for even a day.

PLANTING

Sometimes you will plant new seeds. There will be times for gentle pruning and times for daring transplants. Be aware, alert and vital. Respond to what you hear and see. Do not drift through life. Live every day as if it were your last and every minute as if it were your first.

XXVIII

GIFTS

From time to time you will experience some-thing out of the ordinary. Perhaps it is a con-tinual part of you—a particular talent or ability that you have. Or, there will be brief moments of deep stillness. Then again you may suddenly find that you have surprising strength and ability in a particu-lar situation.

These are all gifts, little treasures that help you know your nature. You are a royal child who is often out wandering in the mud. If you forget your nature you may wander aimlessly until a few days or hours before your death. Gifts are being sent to you all the time as daily reminders of your nature. The frantic people who are always protecting themselves and trying to insure their future are seldom aware of these gifts. They are so focused on what they do not have that they overlook what they already possess.

Sometimes there is a special gift. Often it comes after a time of great spiritual dryness. You have been a caterpillar for a long time. You feel deserted. You cannot find your inner light. You are arid and alone. Your cocoon seems a dull prison. You can give up and it is all over. Or something inside of you will say, "Do not abandon the years of daily disci-pline. Purge yourself. Purify yourself." The moment when you cannot see that it is doing you any good is the most important time for discipline. Experience the aloneness. Be still. Travel up your inner moun-tain for several days. Gradually without your know-ing it a spiritual conversion may take place. It is so natural you will not even notice. Your petty nature is being replaced by your royal nature. You will come down from the mountain and continue life.

There may come a moment when a flaming arrow pierces your heart. You see everything the way it really is, you are frightened and tempted to hold back, to be safe. If you do the experience ends. But if your time on the mountain has taught you a toler-ance for uncertainty you will let go. You will spin in wildness. Tears and laughter will be all the same. You will want to burst. There is no time. There is no space. There is no life. There is no death.

You are burning. You are no longer looking at the flame. You are the flame! Gradually you will stop spinning but you have broken your cocoon. You are a butterfly. Now you must be still and let your wings dry. Be wary of pride. The gift is not for you alone. It reminds others of their nature. Despite the inner ex-plosion your experience will seem routine; move toward the routineness. Avoid specialness and ad-miration. You are to be a note in a song; listen for the song.

While your wings are drying you will again feel alone. You will want to deny the experience and try to crawl back into the cocoon. You are not alone. You are more connected to life than ever before. Now, spread your wings and fly.

You are in the same world as before but now you can really see it and feel it. Now life is in you and you are in life. All is at home. All is one. There is a light within you. Let your light shine.

XXIX

SIMPLICITY

The essence of harmonious living is to stop questing after things that are hard to obtain.

Learn to distinguish between doing the natural thing and doing the proper thing. To use common plants from your back yard to make a tea is one thing. To search all over the world for the finest examples of these plants and to make your tea from an imported, handsomely packaged and expensive product is quite another matter.

A tree does not fret over the lack of the best environment or lament the lack of the finest nutrients. A tree uses what is at hand.

Living the simple life means moving into nature's house rather than trying to crowd all of nature into a spare guest room in your house. It is important for you never to lose your sense of awe of your host. It is equally important for you to always feel at home. Maintaining this balance is not difficult so long as you leave your self-love at the gate.

Begin by getting rid of the things you do not need. You have only one mouth so you have no use for five cups. You pay dearly for housing and caring for all the things you do not need.

Next, discover all the things you can do for yourself. Re-discover your vitality. Use the energy you waste on attempting to get others to do things for you to do those things yourself. In this way you will begin to learn the workings of things and the interconnectedness within the community of life.

Then ground yourself: put down roots. A frequently transplanted tree will not survive. Give up your supposed freedom to move around, to decide things for yourself, to secure your future. Only then will you awaken to the simplicity and the strength within you.

There are no tourists in the land of the simple life, only permanent residents. All a dilettante experiences is a costume party. A commitment is needed before you can see this country. The commitment is to develop an attitude of evenness, to take all as it comes. Do not assume you know what is bad for you and what is good for you.

The simple life is breathing in unison with the day. Everything that comes to you each day is a gift. Use it all. Do not strive for anything more. Simply improve the gifts you have received. It is enough.

XXX

THE PILGRIMAGE

When you were born you joined a wagon train. The train has been traveling for a long time and when you die it will still go on traveling.

At night when you sleep, or during the day at moments of stillness, you are completely involved in the journey. At other times you become so concerned with petty things that you lose track of the journey. Yet, you never completely forget. You were born to make this journey and it is only in this venture that your soul will find true rest.

You are a pilgrim. Perhaps there is some destination for this wagon train, but you will never know it. Learn from an apple tree. This tree may be a chapter in a story leading to some entirely new type of tree. But it is enough for this tree to be itself, to go through the cycles of the seasons, to live and to die. So it is for you. The destination is the pilgrimage itself. Here is where you will live and die.

Each generation loses a little more awareness of the journey. The baby carried on her mother's back knew that stillness and movement go together. But you have forgotten stillness. A child listening to a river knew that the river goes ever on. But you have forgotten how to listen.

You and your brothers and sisters have wasted your time in being successful. At times you have pulled the whole wagon train over and just lain around doing nothing. You make a virtue of vices. You seek ways to avoid work and as a result you grow limp and flabby. Then you complain that life is dull and meaningless. You try to amuse yourself by pouring your vital energy into unimportant things. Your worst offense is that you make life more diffi- cult for those who one day will take your place. You focus your attention on how your children can affect you. By your example, you should be helping them to find their relationship to the wagon train and to the journey.

So get on your feet and get moving. The longer you lie around the harder it is to get up. There will be problems, but they can only be discussed when you are moving in the rhythm of the journey. If you stop to handle a problem you become the problem.

Keep moving. Look at what is around you. Give up your petty desires and goals. Empty out. Keep moving. You will feel your strength return.

When you finally move you sometimes act as if you were carrying the torch out to the great un- known. You are wrong. Others have carried the torch out. Now you are carrying it back. You are re- turning. Accept your homeless home. Give up any other ideas. You are not a stranger in a foreign place. There is no place that is more your home than where you are now. You are a stranger in your own homeland. The earth beneath you knows you. Heaven above you knows you. All that is around you is welcoming you. There should be no strangers here. You and the grass are one. You and the bird are one. You and the path are one. You and the wagon train are one. You and the rhythm are one.

You are the pilgrimage. The pilgrimage is you.

Tolbert McCarroll is Elder of the Community of the Simple Life, a small, contemplative religious order of men and women located at the monastic farm "Starcross" in Annapolis, Sonoma County, California. Although in the Christian tradition, the Community draws from the spiritual teachings and practices of all cultures. Brother Tolbert is a spiritual teacher for a growing number of questing people around the country. He approaches the spiritual path with the firmness of a Zen master and the gentleness of an older brother.

After receiving his doctorate in 1955, Brother Tolbert embarked on a unique career that has allowed him to build bridges between Eastern and Western spiritual traditions, and to find links between contemporary psychology and religious experience. The main focus of his spiritual direction is to relate the teachings of the ancients to everyday life. He guides himself and others toward more freedom through less self-centeredness.

In addition to his primary work, Brother Tolbert is regularly associated with a number of educational, religious, governmental and community institutions. He was the Founder of the Humanist Institute. His deep love of contemplative spirituality has not led him to the life of a recluse. Among his students are people in every walk of life looking for inner nourishment. Brother Tolbert is equally at home on the tractor, at the podium, in the ghetto, on television, in a contemplative monastery, the classroom, or a Juvenile Court. In recent years he has worked with terminally ill people, helped provide a home for neglected children, and become involved in the needs of rural people.

Brother Tolbert is the author of the well-received work, EXPLORING THE INNER WORLD, A GUIDEBOOK FOR PERSONAL GROWTH AND RENEWAL, Signet.

Chris Smith